Milady's Hairstyling

The Styling Guide
Men's, Women's and Children's Styles
to accompany Milady's Haircutting

Kenneth Young

Milady Publishing Company
(A Division of Delmar Publishers, Inc.)
3 Columbia Circle, Box 12519
Albany, New York 12212-2519

PUBLISHER: Catherine Frangie

ILLUSTRATOR: Robert Richards

PRODUCTION: John Mickelbank

For information address:
Milady Publishing Company
(A Division of Delmar Publishers Inc.)
3 Columbia Circle, Box 12519
Albany, New York 12212-2519

Printed in the United States of America
Published simultaneously in Canada
by Nelson Canada
a division of The Thomson Corporation

1 2 3 4 5 6 7 8 9 10   XXX   99 98 97 96 95 94 93

ISBN 1-56253-154-9

Library of Congress Catalog Card Number: 93-26198

Directions for Use of This Book

This working manual was created in order to give you real life practice in styling hair. The technicals in this book are actual renditions of salon styles that the author has created for his clients.

Each technical is designed to give you practice working on a specific type of style, and different types of hair. *Milady's Hairstyling* includes men's, women's, and children's styles ranging from the conservative to the trendy. You will get practice using the blowdryer, an assortment of brushes, and styling aids.

There is also an implements key that will help you determine which implement you will need to use.

The last page of the book contains a scoring guide for your instructor's evaluation of your performance of these techniques.

Keep practicing each until you are comfortable enough to add your own unique elements to the finished style. After you have mastered these styling techniques you will be well prepared for the hairstyling challenges you will encounter in your professional salon life. Enjoy and remember—never stop learning.

Implements Key

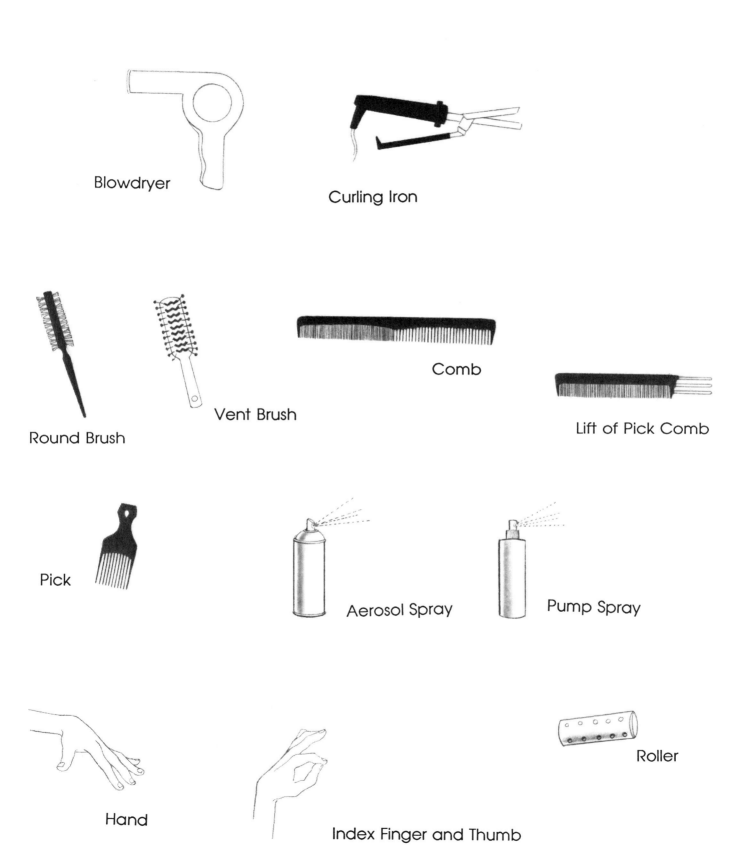

Blowdryer

Curling Iron

Round Brush

Vent Brush

Comb

Lift of Pick Comb

Pick

Aerosol Spray

Pump Spray

Hand

Index Finger and Thumb

Roller

Style

1

2

Style 1

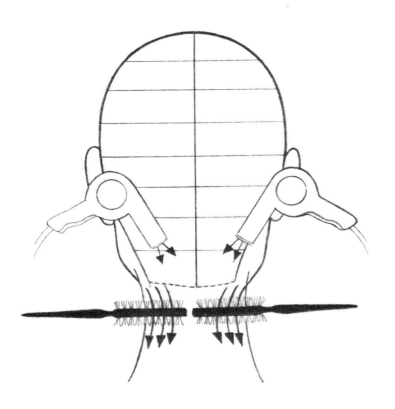

A

Towel dry hair, then remove approximately 80 percent of the moisture with blowdryer. Part the hair down the middle from forehead to crown. Use a round brush approximately 1 1/2 to 2 inches in diameter to create this style. Divide the back into two sections from the top of the crown to the nape. Using partings the same width as your round brush, place brush at the scalp and move the brush through the hair, follow the brush with blowdryer from scalp to ends. When the hair is almost completely dry, roll the hair from the ends to the scalp. Direct the air to the top and bottom of the brush. Allow hair to cool for 10 seconds before removing the brush to lock in the set.

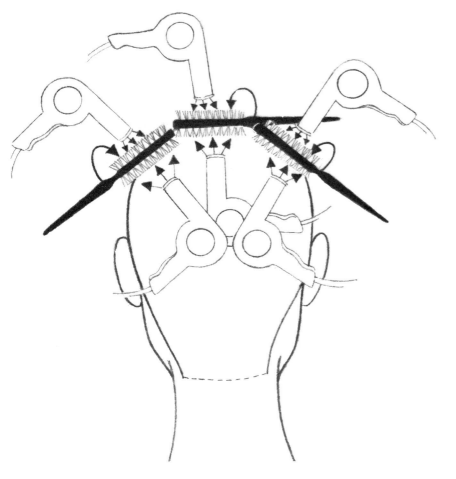

B

Starting in the center, take a section of hair the length and width of the brush at the top of the crown. Over direct the hair 45 degrees forward toward the face. Roll the hair around the brush from the ends to the scalp. Direct the dryer to both the front and back of the brush. Allow the hair to cool, then remove the brush. Repeat the same procedure on the sides of the crown to create volume and fullness in the crown area.

Style 1

C

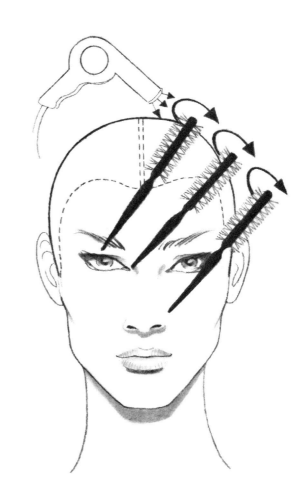

Starting at ear level on one side, take a section once again the same width as the brush. When the hair is almost dry, wrap the hair around the brush from the ends to the scalp. Direct the heat at the top and bottom of brush. Allow the hair to cool and remove the brush. Follow this procedure until entire side is dry. This will create a soft wave around the face and fullness at the part.

D

Follow the same procedure on the other side of the head. Start at the bottom of the section and work towards the top making sure to allow each curl to cool before removing the brush.

4

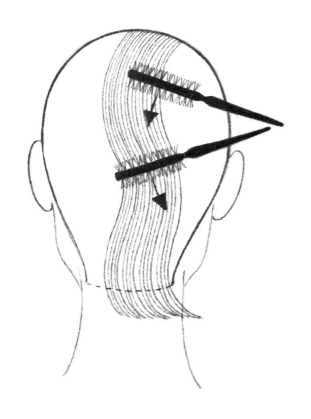

E

To comb out the back of this style, use a vent-type brush or large tooth comb. The hair will fall into soft horizontal waves. Follow the direction of the waves with the brush. Brushing or combing the hair should be light, and used only to create direction. Over brushing will relax the wave. For added fullness in the crown, lightly backbrush the top of the crown before brushing in the waves.

F

Brush the sides back and away from the face starting at the forehead. Brush the next wave using a diagonal line forward and then back. Continue to brush in the waves on both sides using diagonal lines. Use your brush or comb to turn the ends under.

NOTE: Depending on the texture and natural curl of the hair, you may need to use a liquid styling aid to hold the waves.

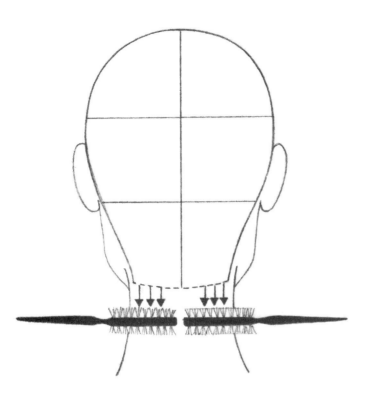

A

Towel dry well and use blowdryer until hair is about 80 percent dry. Use either a vent brush or a round brush when drying this style. Start in the back and divide the head into two sections. Make your partings the same width as the brush. Dry the hair from the scalp to the ends. Direct the air from your dryer away from the scalp towards the ends. The dryer should follow the brush. Begin in the nape and work up the back of each section until all the hair is dry.

B

To dry the front of this style, all the hair will be directed towards the face. Begin at the hair line at the temple. Take a vertical parting of hair. Direct the hair forward, onto the face. Dry the hair from the scalp to the ends. Work up the parting toward the bang area (do not dry the bang area now). Continue to dry the sides working from the front to the back. Repeat this procedure on both sides. When the sides are completed, start at the hairline in the bang section. Divide this section into two partings. The first parting will be dried from roots to ends. Over direct the second parting toward the back of the head with the ends curled forward. This will create height in the bang area.

Style 2

C

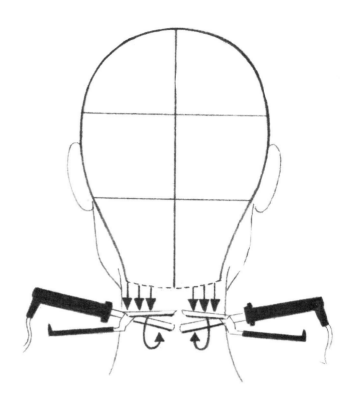

Using a 3/4-inch curling iron, start in the back to give the hair an end curl. Make sure the hair winds around the iron only one full turn. The hair will be curled under. Follow the same sectioning and partings used in blow drying the hair to complete the back section.

D

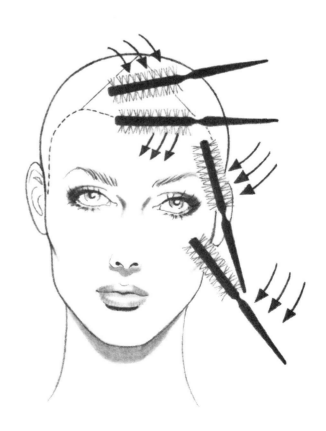

On the sides and top, we will be following the same pattern as the blow dry. Make a 2-inch side part on the left side of the head. To curl the sides, comb the hair forward using vertical parts. You will use an end curl on the sides, one complete turn around the curling iron. All the hair will be curled under. Start at the hairline and work your way up the parting. Then work from front to back. Repeat on the opposite side. To curl the top, we will use an end curl on both partings.

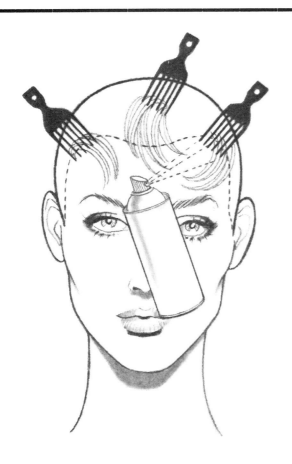

E

Use a pick to finish this style. Start at the top in the bang section. Place the pick in the hair behind the curl. Lift the curl away from the head. While lifting, spray the hair with a medium to strong hold spray. This will maintain volume and separation of the curl. Repeat this procedure on the sides lifting the curl away from the head and spraying. To accent the style, gently pull small strands of hair from the hairline toward the face and spray into place.

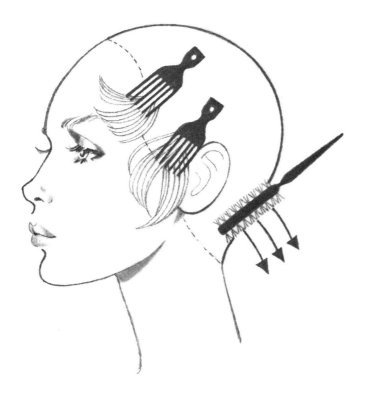

F

Brush the back down and turn under. Remember not to over brush the hair as this will relax the curl. Use a pick to lift the hair away from the head in the nape and spray lightly. This will create additional volume in the perimeter, at the back.

Style 3

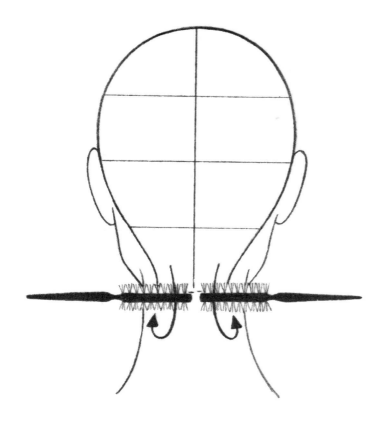

A

Remove moisture from the hair with blowdryer. Use a 1 1/2-inch to 2-inch round brush to dry the hair and set the style. Begin by dividing the back into two sections vertically. You will be working with partings in each section the width of the brush. Dry the hair from roots to ends. When the hair is dry, roll the hair around the brush. Direct the heat from the dryer at the top and bottom of the brush. Allow to cool before removing the brush. Repeat this procedure on both sides of the back.

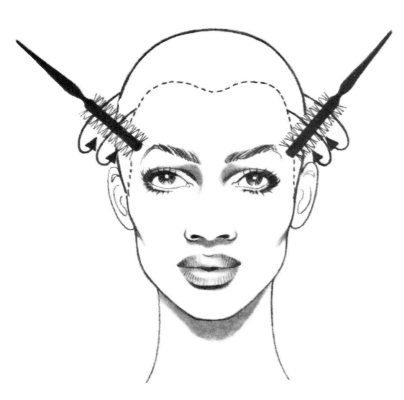

B

Use the same technique on the side sections. Dry from the roots to the ends first then roll the brush up to the scalp. Heat the hair on both sides and allow to cool before removing. It is best to have several brushes of the same size when using this technique to save time. You can dry another parting while a completed parting is cooling.

Style 3

C

Divide the bang section into two. Over direct the hair away from the direction of the style will move. The brush will be sitting directly on base. Dry the hair on both sides of the brush. Be sure not to direct the heat at the scalp. When the hair is cool, remove the brush.

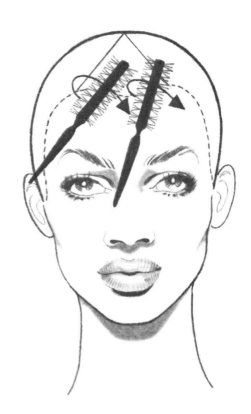

D

Use a 1-inch curling iron to curl just the ends. Place the iron at the ends of the hair around the perimeter. Turn the iron one revolution only, more than one revolution around the iron will make it difficult to control the ends. Follow the same procedure in the bang section, one turn at the ends.

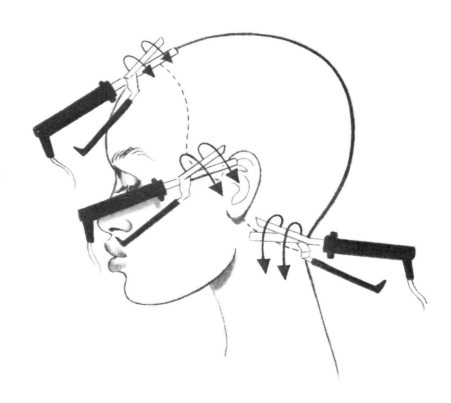

E

Lightly backcomb the hair in the bang section to help support the height. Lightly backbrush the sides and back from the underside of the style. This will create more volume above the perimeter line.

F

Gently lift the ends of bangs with a pick to the desired height. While lifting, spray with a medium to firm hold spray. Do not over comb the bangs as this will remove the backcombing needed to support the bangs. Use a brush with soft bristles to delicately brush the sides and back. Make sure the bristles of the brush do not penetrate into the hair as this will remove the back brushing and decrease the volume.

A

Prepare the hair using a sculpting lotion or gel. Place the gel from the scalp to 2 inches out from the scalp. Bend the head over, then direct the flow of air from the dryer towards the scalp. You will be drying the hair against its natural fall. This will create volume throughout the style. Start at the top of the back section then work down. Do not dry the ends as this will cause the hair to frizz.

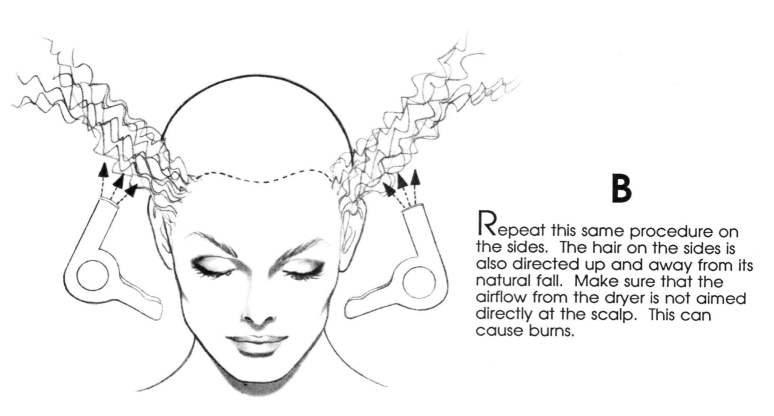

B

Repeat this same procedure on the sides. The hair on the sides is also directed up and away from its natural fall. Make sure that the airflow from the dryer is not aimed directly at the scalp. This can cause burns.

Style 4

C

After drying the back and sides, return the head to an upright position. Use your fingers at the hair line in the temples to lift and direct the hair up and away from the face. Once again, only dry the scalp area.

D

Start at the back of the bang section. Dry the hair at the scalp area using your fingers to lift the hair. Work from back to the front. At the hair line direct the hair back and away from the face.

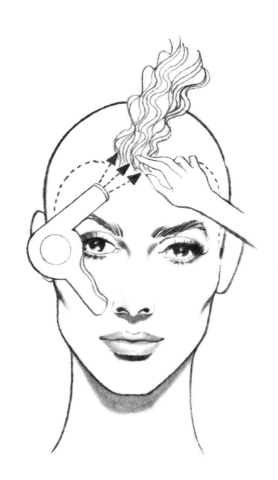

E

Tilt the head down. Lift the hair in the back using either your fingers or a pick and spray with a liquid sculpting lotion. Work from the top of the head to the bottom. The spray on damp hair will create separation and hold the curl.

F

Keeping the head in a down position spray the sides with sculpting lotion starting at the top of the side section. Make sure the spray covers the entire length of the hair strand. Return the head to its natural position to finish the top. Start at the back of the top section. Lift and spray with the sculpting lotion. Continue towards the front. At the hairline give the hair direction to the side by gently lifting the hair to the side and spraying.

5

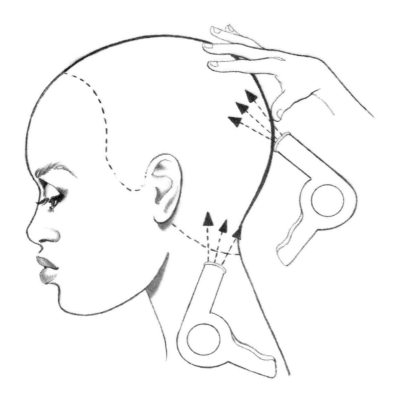

A

Work a light or medium hold styling lotion throughout the hair. You will be using a diffuser or a blowdryer on low speed to create this style and maintain the curl. Use your fingers instead of a brush to keep from over separating the curl. Start drying at the top of the crown gently lifting the hair away from the head and over to one side. Complete the entire crown, then dry the nape. If the hair is too short in the nape to lift with the fingers, direct the dryer up and allow the airflow to lift the hair.

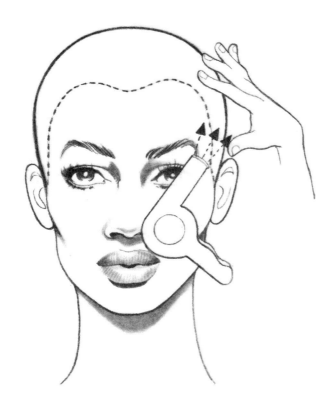

B

Start at the temple on the heavy side. Use your fingers to direct the hair away from the face. As the hair dries, move up the side of face, always drying wet hair onto dry hair. Once again, if the hair is too short, allow the airflow from the dryer to move the hair back.

Style 5

C

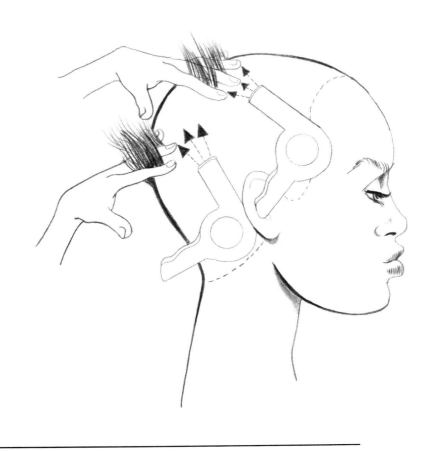

The hair on the light side will move diagonally up and back. Direct the airflow from the dryer at a 45 degree angle up and towards the back. Again, start at the back of the side section and work from the back to the front.

D

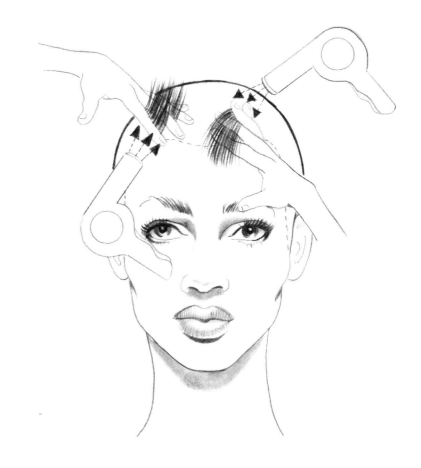

Divide the top into two sections. The first section is from the outer corner of the right eye to the center of the nose. From the center of the nose draw a diagonal line to the left side of the top. This will leave a triangle section on the left side of the top. This section will be dried starting at the hairline and directed gently forward over the left eye. Continue drying the hair directing it forward until the entire section is dry. The remaining hair in the right section will be dried diagonally back from the right side to the left side.

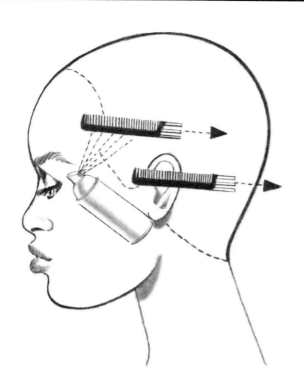

E

Mist the hair very lightly with water. This will cause the curl to reform and reactivate the sculpting lotion. Use a pick comb to gently direct the hair on the sides from the front to the back. Comb the hair in the back from the nape up to the crown.

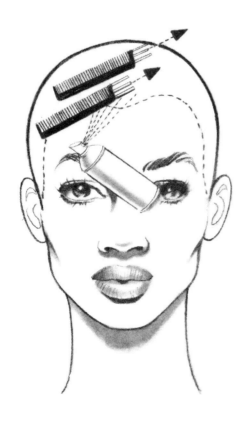

F

Gently comb the hair on top using a pick diagonally across the top from right to left. Pull the hair down over the left eye. Spray the hair with a sculpting spray or hairspray to hold the curls in place.

6

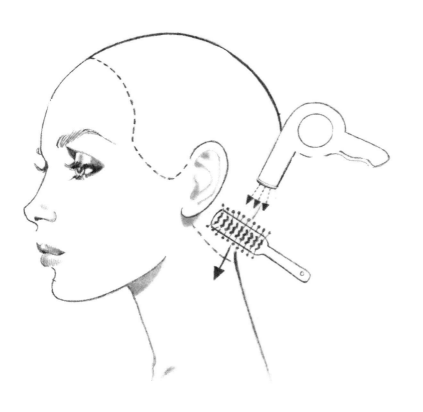

A

Use a blowdryer to dry the short hair at the nape. Direct the hair down starting at the hairline. Then work up the nape to the occipital bone. Dry the entire nape area before starting the crown.

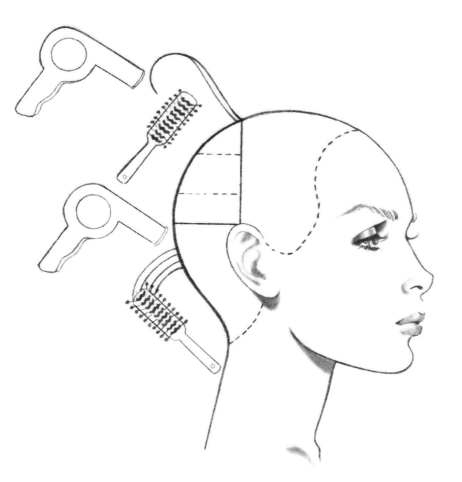

B

Start at the bottom of the crown. Use sections the width of the brush. Dry the hair under using a vent brush. Be sure to dry from the scalp to the ends. As you work up to the top section, direct the hair away from the scalp at a 90 degree angle. This will create volume and lift.

Style 6

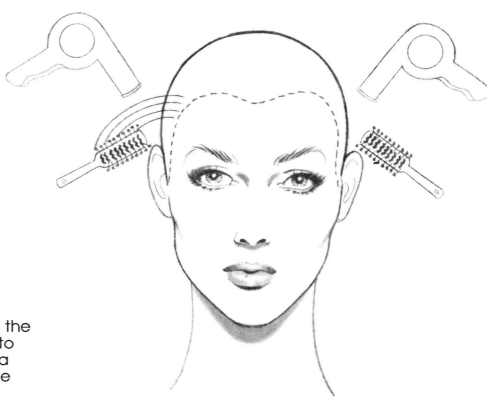

C

Dry the side sections same as the crown. Work from the bottom to the top. Direct the hair out at a 90 degree angle to increase the volume at the sides.

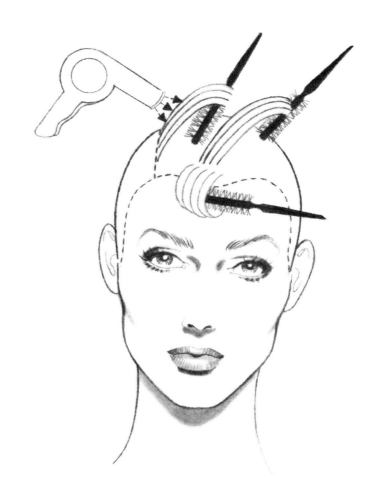

D

Create a side part over the right eye. Make a diagonal bang section 1 inch deep at the part to the corner of the left eye. Dry the hair in the bang section under using your vent brush. In the top section, section dry the hair using a large round brush (2-inch diameter or more). Over direct the hair around the brush to create height and fullness in the top section. Dry from the scalp to the ends. Then set the brush on base, heat the hair from both sides. Allow the hair to cool then remove the brush.

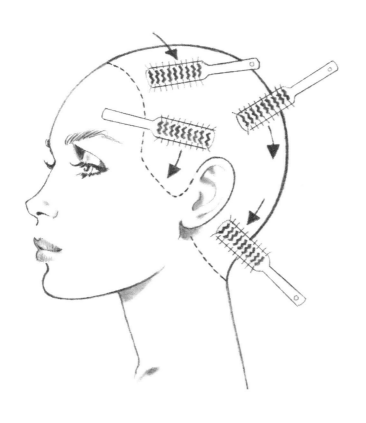

E

Once dry brush all the hair smooth and close to the head. Do not include the bang section when brushing. Start in the nape and then work towards the top. Brush the sides down and the top across the head away from the part. Make sure all the hair blends smoothly around the head.

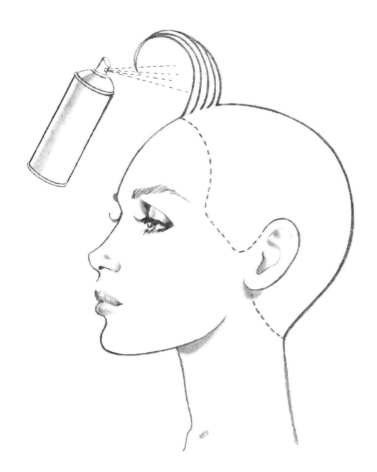

F

With the thumb and the index finger gently lift the hair just behind the bang section to a height of 1 1/2 to 2 inches. Use a pick to smooth and blend this area into the side. Spray the hair with a medium holding spray. For volume use your vent brush to lift the sides and back at the perimeter.

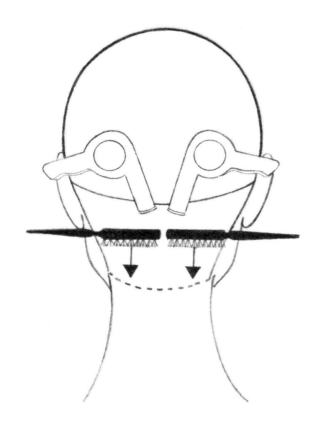

A

Blow dry the hair in the nape down and into its natural growth pattern. Do not try to change the direction the hair moves naturally, this will cause the hair to standout from the head.

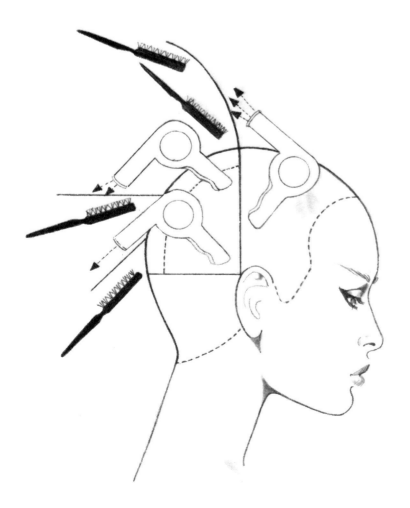

B

To dry the crown, divide the back of the head into three vertical sections and beginning with the center section start at the bottom. Using partings the diameter of the brush, dry the hair from the scalp to the ends. Dry the lower section at a 45-degree angle and as you move up the back gradually increase the angle to 90 degrees from the head until you reach the top of the crown. Turn the ends under by bending the hair with the brush just before the strand is dry. Dry the entire center section first then dry the side sections.

Style 7

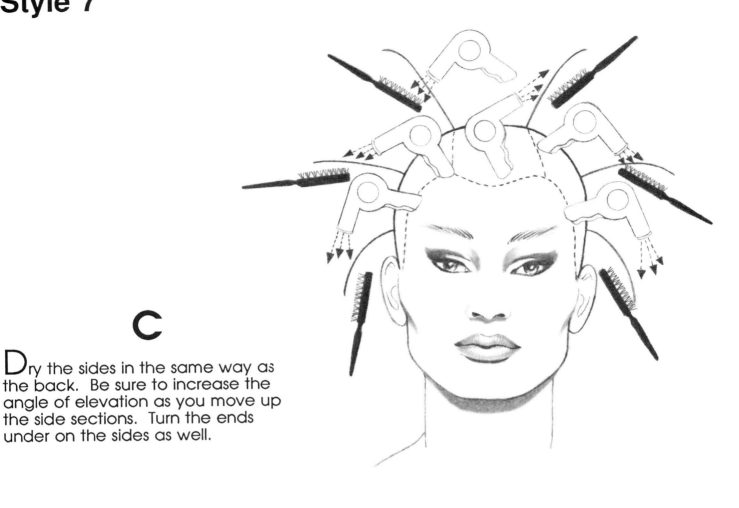

C

Dry the sides in the same way as the back. Be sure to increase the angle of elevation as you move up the side sections. Turn the ends under on the sides as well.

D

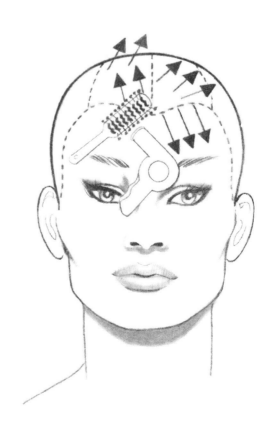

Use a gel or sculpting lotion in the bangs to support the hair. The bang section will be divided into two parts, the left and the right sides. Dry the right side at the hairline straight out from the head. As you work toward the back of the bang section decrease the angle and direct the hair back. This will help to blend the bang into the crown. Decrease the drying angle on the left side of the bang gradually from the center of the bang section to the side. At the hairline, dry approximately a 1 inch thick parting, over the eye.

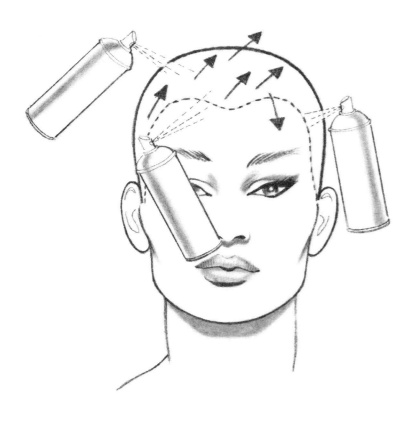

E

Use your thumb and index finger to separate the hair in the bang section. Try holding a small amount of hair and gently snapping your fingers to create an uncontrived look. Use an aerosol finishing spray to maintain the soft spiky look.

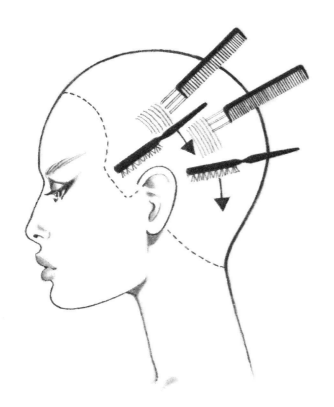

F

Brush the sides and back for control and smoothness. Turn all the ends under using your brush, by brushing the hair from underneath. Gently blend a small amount of hair in the perimeter of the bank section, into the heavy side and the back.

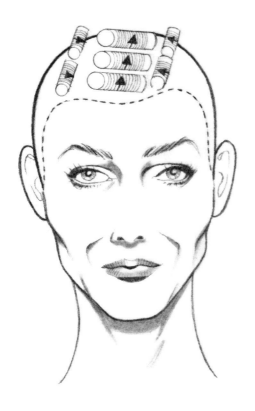

A

Saturate the hair with a crisp hold setting or sculpting lotion. Place rollers on base and set straight back in the top section. Use small diameter rollers throughout the set to create lots of curl. Roll one roller on each side of the top, up towards the center row.

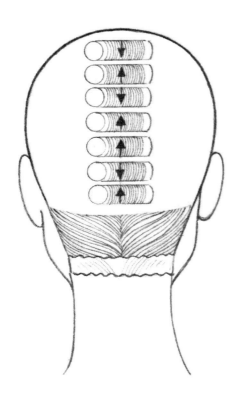

B

Continue the top rollers into the back section stopping at the nape. Roll one roller down and the next roller up alternating to the bottom of the row. This will help to create an explosion of curls. Brush the hair down in the center of the nape. Then brush the sides of the nape to the center. Secure with hair tape.

Style 8

C

Roll the left side straight back. The rollers will be placed vertically. Roll all the way to the center row in the back. You will need to use two rows of rollers to fill the side section. Set the rollers on base. Slightly drag the hair up and around the rollers on the sides. This will give the hair a slight upward movement as it is directed back.

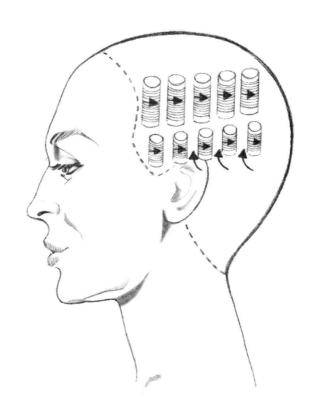

D

Repeat the same procedure on the right side.

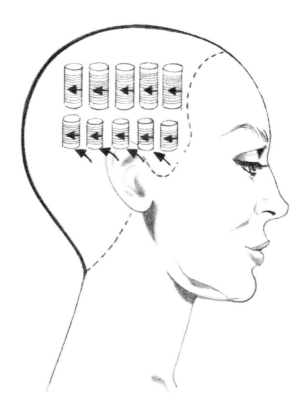

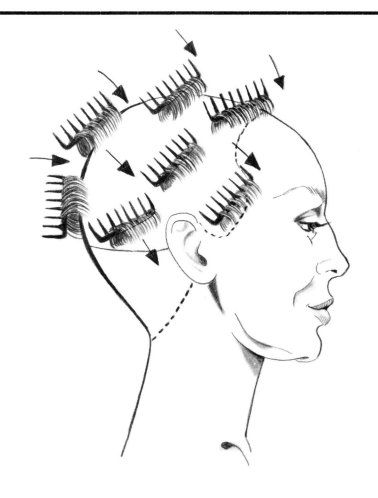

E

Break down the set using your fingers or a wide tooth comb. Do not brush the hair before back combing. Back comb all the hair with the exception of the nape. Be sure to pack a back comb base 2 inches deep. If the hair is slick and will not back comb easily, spray the hair with hair spray first.

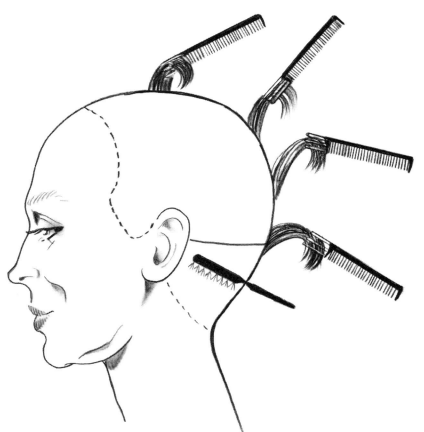

F

Brush the nape hair using a soft bristle brush. Brush the center of the nape down and the sides of the nape into the center. Spray the nape to hold the hair in place. Use your pick comb to lift the ends of the hair and direct the curl towards the back. Start lifting at the center and bottom of the crown. Work up to the top and center hairline. Repeat the same procedure starting at the sides at the bottom of the crown. Direct the hair back and blend into the center section from the nape to the front. Be sure not to over comb the hair. The look is casual and curly.

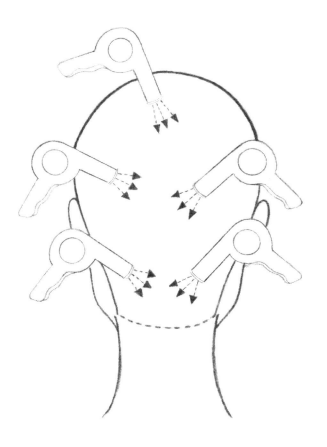

A

Dry the nape and crown area directing the hair towards the center. Start at the hair line and work up to the top. At the top of the crown direct the hair straight back pulling the hair up and away to create volume.

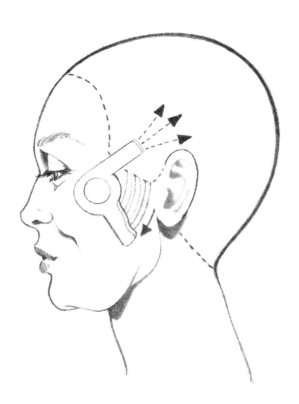

B

Next dry the left side. Start at the back of the side and work towards the front. Dry the hair directing it diagonally back and up. Dry a small amount of hair below the temple, at the sideburn, towards the face.

Style 9

C

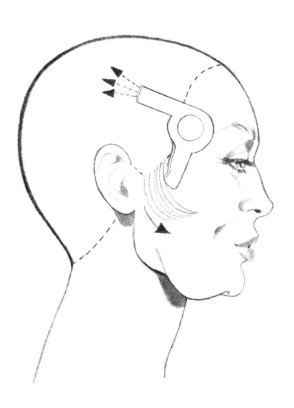

Repeat the same procedure on the right side. Be sure to start at the back of the section and work to the front hairline.

D

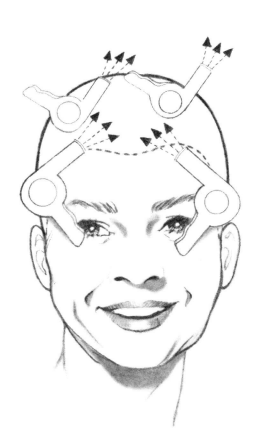

Dry the top section diagonally back and from right to left. Start at the back of the section and work to the front. Be sure each parting of hair is dry before moving on to the next. Over the left eye, at hairline, dry the hair straight back. This will create a slight wave at the front hairline.

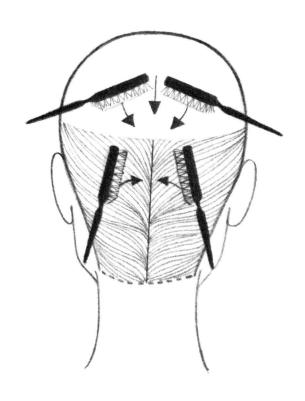

E

Brush the hair in the nape and lower third of the crown into the center. This will create a line down the center of the back. Brush the center of the crown down and the sides diagonally to the center to blend the hair into the center.

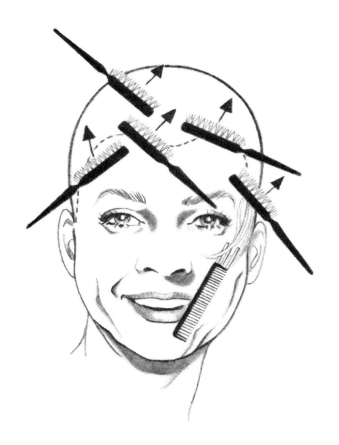

F

Start on the sides and brush the hair back into the crown. Brush the top diagonally back from the right to the left. Brush the hair up at the hairline and spray. Then take the small section dried forward and wisp the hair using a pick comb or your fingers.

10

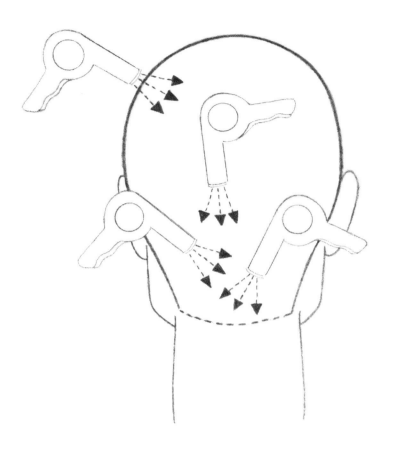

A

Dry the hair in the nape and crown area down. At the top of the crown dry the longer hair diagonally from left to right.

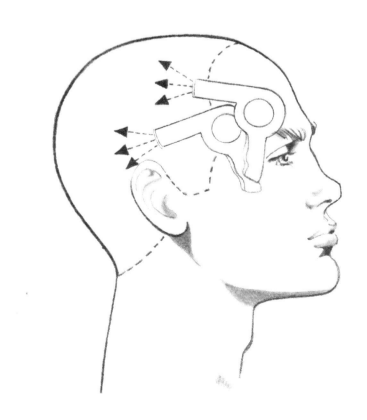

B

Dry the longer hair at the top of right side (light side) diagonally back and up. This will give a spiky effect at the part. Dry the short area diagonally down and back.

C

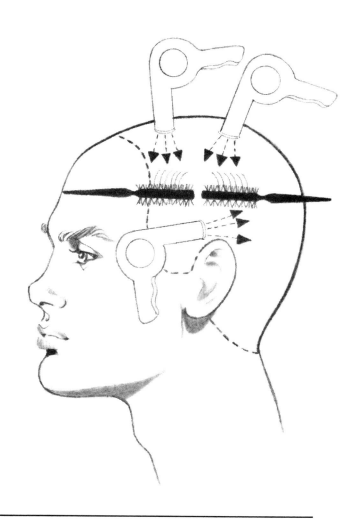

Dry the long hair on top across the head from right to left using a vent brush. Turn the ends of the hair under as you dry. Do not try to create volume at the top. Dry the shorter hair diagonally back and down.

D

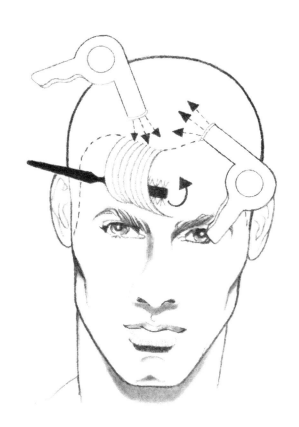

Dry the scalp area over the right eye up and back from the face to create height over the right eye. Then dry the ends of the right side and the left side of the bangs under. This will create a wave over the left eye.

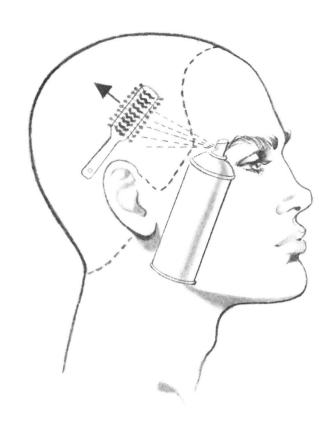

E

Using a vent brush or your fingers, lift the hair up on the right side and spray with a strong holding spray.

F

Smooth the top and bang section using a comb or brush from right to left. Then take your comb and place at the bottom of the weight line at the back of the head. Run the comb along the weight line towards the face. This will make the line more definite. Then using your thumb and index finger lift a section of the hair 1 inch deep into the hairline over the right eye. Spray the bang with a firm holding finishing spray.

11

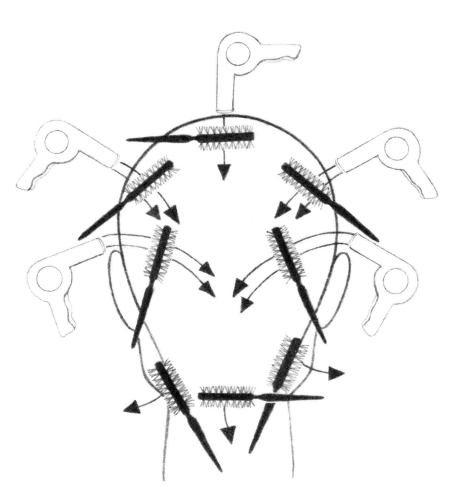

A

Remove most of the moisture from the hair before starting to create direction in the blow dry. Start at the perimeter of the nape. Dry the center down and under. Then dry the sides of the perimeter of the nape forward and under. Dry the rest of the hair in the back towards center working up to the top of the head. At the top of the back section dry the hair back.

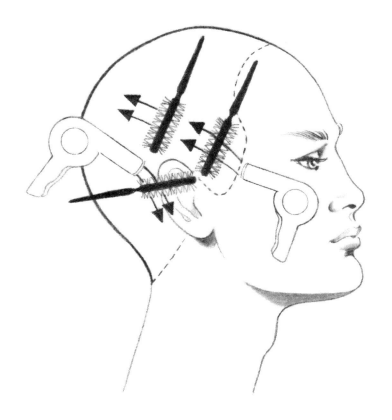

B

On the right side in the perimeter over the ear, dry a section approximately 1 inch deep straight down and under. Then starting at the back of the side section dry the hair diagonally up and back. Work forward to the hairline.

Style 11

C

Repeat the same procedure on the left side as on the right. Dry the hair over the ear under to give control at the perimeter when we comb the hair back.

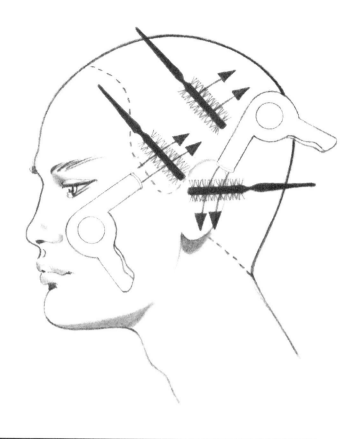

D

Starting at the back of the top section dry the hair diagonally back lifting the hair away from the head to create some height. Work from the back towards the front hair line. At the hair line, over direct the hair back and away from the face.

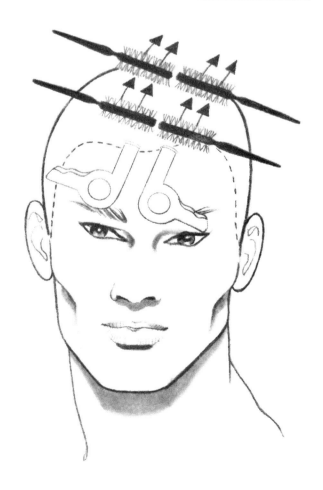

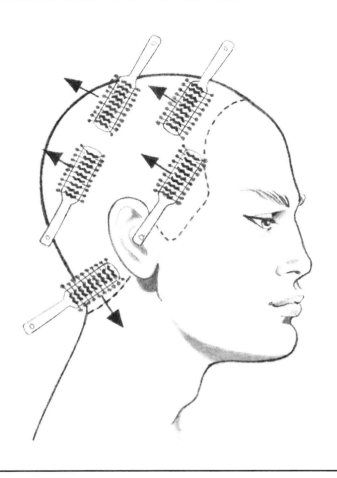

E

Brush the hair in the nape using a vent brush. Turn the hair in the perimeter under in the back. Turn the hair under and towards the front at the sides of the perimeter. Brush the rest of the hair to the center of the back starting at the nape and working to the top. Brush the sides diagonally back and up. Use long strokes and brush from the hairline all the way to the back.

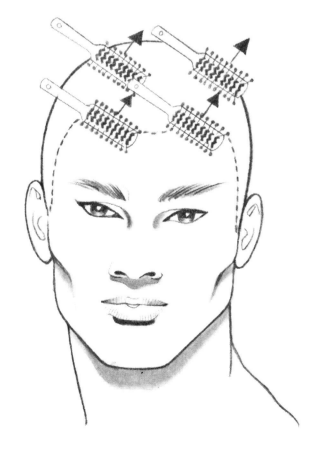

F

Brush all the hair on top at a slight diagonal from right to left. If needed, blend the sides into the top by rebrushing the area between the sides and the top section. Spray with a light hold finishing spray.

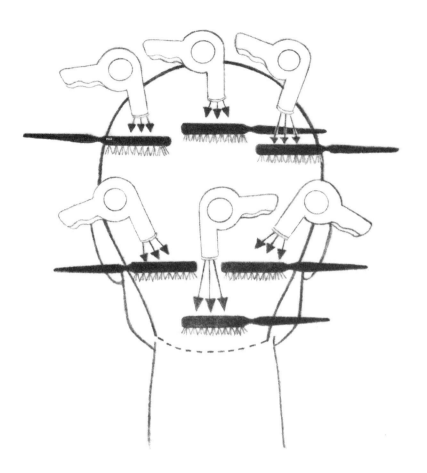

A

Use a blowdryer to dry the hair. Evenly distribute the hair across the top of the crown. Dry all the hair down starting in the nape and continue to the top of the crown.

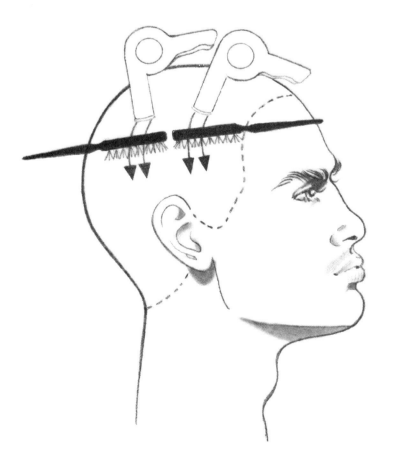

B

On the light side of the part dry the hair straight down. Start over the ear and work up to the part. Do not lift the hair when drying. This style requires the hair to be close to the head. Follow through the hair with the dryer after the brush.

Style 12

C

Dry the heavy side straight down in the same way as the light side.

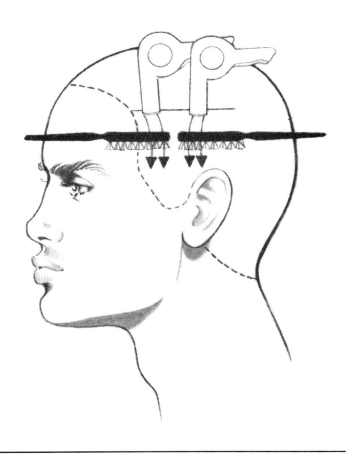

D

Dry the top by brushing across the top section away from the part. Be sure the dryer follows the brush. Start at the back of the top and work forward. If the growth pattern of the hair is towards the face, dry the hair in the bang section diagonally back.

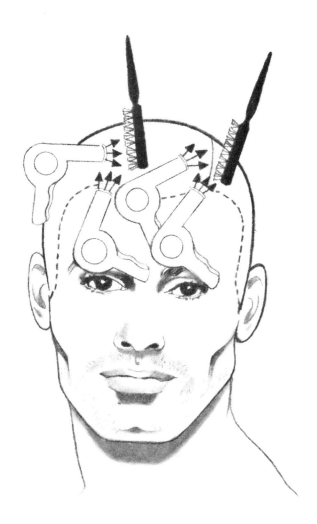

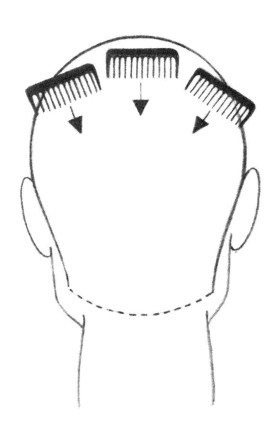

E

Apply a light pomade or styling gel evenly to the hair. Use a styling comb to distribute the hair in the crown. The hair should fan out evenly from the center of the crown.

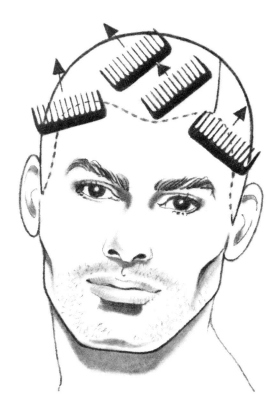

F

Comb the hair on the light side of the part diagonally back and down. Comb the hair on top at the back across the top. Be sure to blend the back of the top section with the top of the crown. Comb the front section of the top diagonally across the head from the part to the heavy side. Finish with a light holding spray.

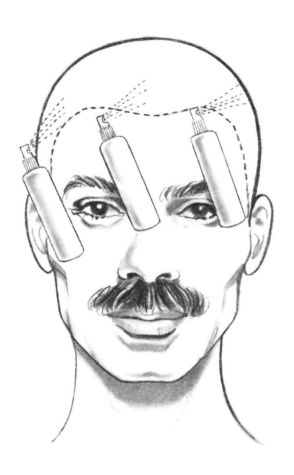

A

Spray the entire head with a soft sculpting spray.

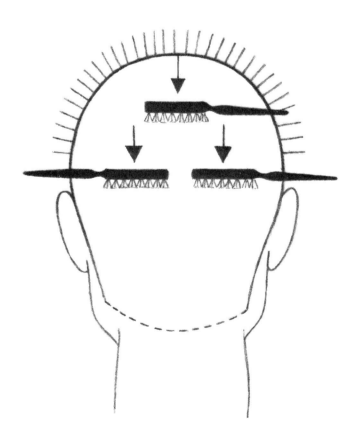

B

Brush the hair down in the back.

Style 13

C

Brush the hair back on the sides. Brush the hair down over the ears.

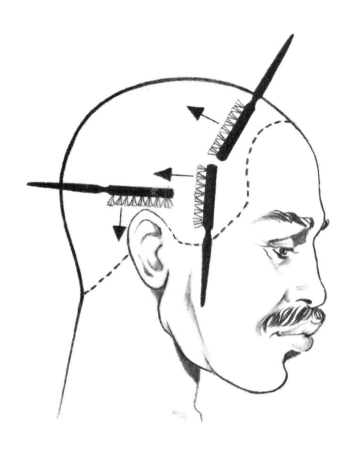

D

Behind the bang section brush the hair straight back. In the longer bang section brush the hair diagonally back and across the head.

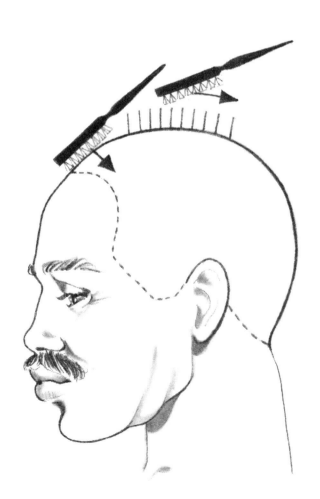

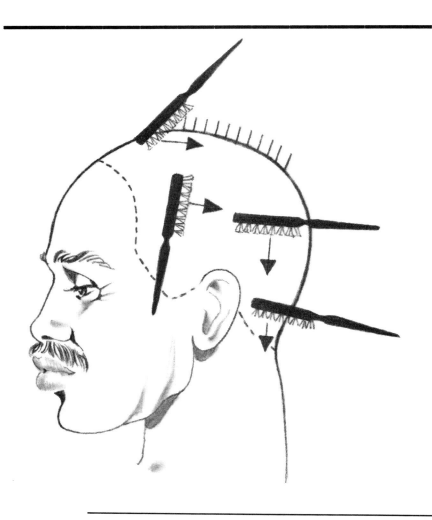

E

After the hair has dried, brush the hair following the same pattern as **A** through **D**. This will soften the hair so as not to look like a gel style.

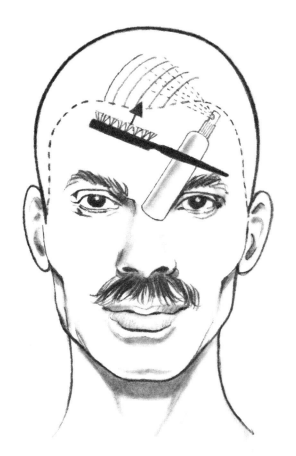

F

Brush the bangs back off the forehead. A light pomade can be used on the bangs to help keep them off the face and make the hair soft.

14

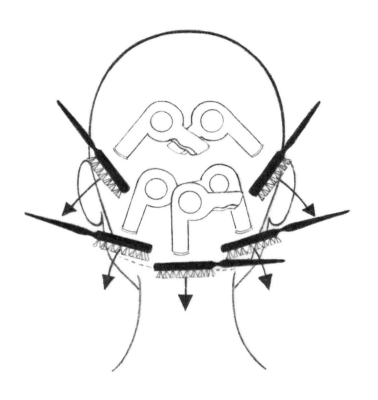

A

Dry the center of the hairline at the nape straight down. Then dry the rest of the back starting at the hairline behind the ear. Work from the hairline back and up to the center of the crown.

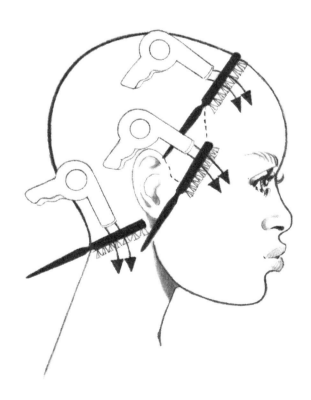

B

Dry the hair at the hairline on the right side towards the face. Then work back directing the hair forward.

Style 14

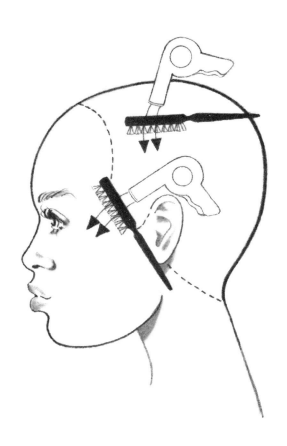

C

On the left side section direct the hair at the temples forward, towards the face. Continue working back on the left side directing the hair forward. Just above the crest line on the left side direct the hair under and down.

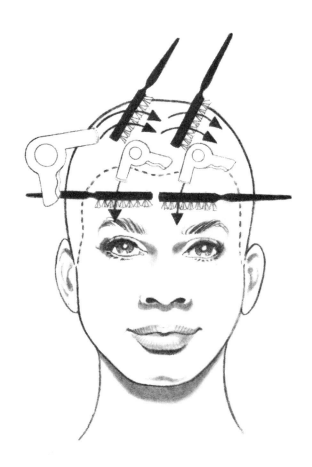

D

Dry a 1 inch deep bang section. Just behind this section, starting on the left side of the top, dry the hair across the top of the head from right to left. Be sure to dry wet hair on to dry hair.

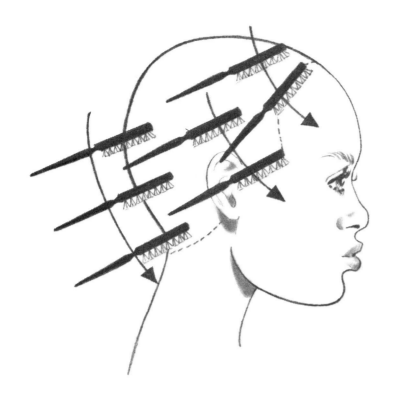

E

Brush the hair from the right center of the back curving down to the hairline just behind the right ear. Brush the hair in the same curving motion starting at the top right side of the crown and moving towards the face just below the right temple. Now brush from the center of the crown and curve down to the right temple.

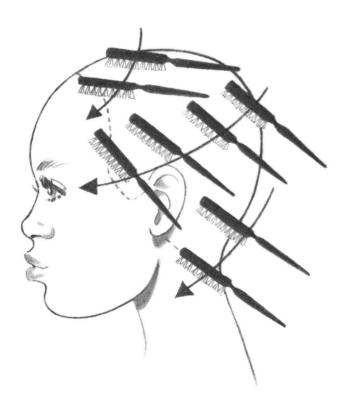

F

On the left side of the back, brush the hair in a curve from the center of the back to the hairline behind the ear. Then brush from the top left side of the crown to just below the left temple. Move to the right side of the top section and brush the hair in a long curve to the left temple. Move forward on the right side of the top and brush in a curve to the area over the corner of the left eye.

15

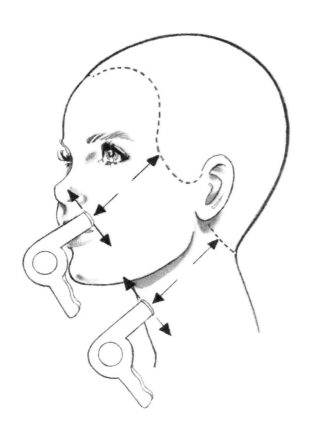

A

Dry the hair up and away from the head to create a full fluffy look. Start in the center of the back. Dry the hair in the nape first, then work up to the top. Be sure to keep the blowdryer moving and about 8 inches away from the head to avoid burning the scalp.

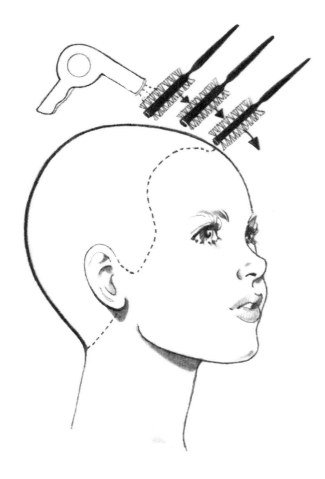

B

Dry the bang area using a 1 1/2 inch diameter round brush. Divide the bangs into three horizontal partings. Dry the parting at the hairline off base. The middle parting will be dried on a 1/2 base and the third parting will be dried on base.

Style 15

C

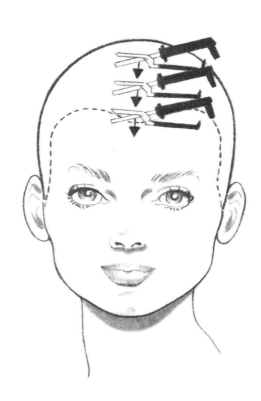

Use a medium barrel curling iron (3/4 inch) to curl the ends of the three partings in the bangs. Wrap the hair one full turn around the iron. Do not roll the hair to the scalp.

D

Use vertical partings starting on the sides to curl the hair. Pull the hair straight out from the head, keeping the hair parallel to the floor. The curling iron will be held vertical and parallel to the partings. Roll one parting forward and one parting back. This will create an explosion of curls. Work from the front to the back. You will have to divide the back into two sections. Separate the nape from the crown. Curl the hair in the back using the same procedure as the sides.

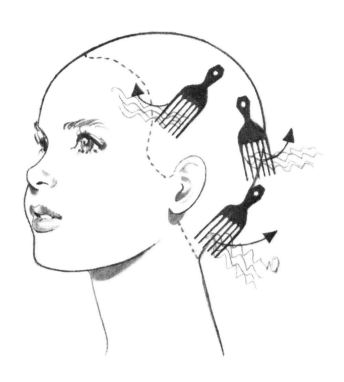

E

Use a pick to lift the curls in the bang up and forward. Then gently pull the front section of the bangs down over the forehead.

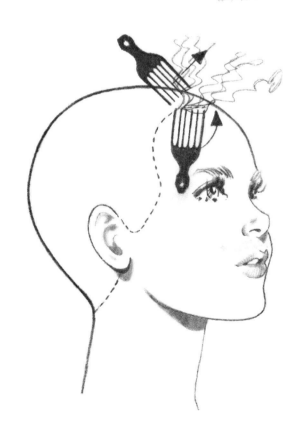

F

Place your pick into the curls. The pick should enter the hair at the scalp and move diagonally up and out from the head. Start at the sides, working from the temple to the back. In the back, lift the nape area first, then the crown. Use a light to medium hold hairspray if needed.

Grading Record

Note: Each time a style is performed, your instructor will grade it on a scale of 1 to 10. A grade of 5 to 6 is average, and any grade below that shows a serious need for improvement.

STYLE 1

Date	Grade	Instructor	Instructor's Comments

STYLE 2

Date	Grade	Instructor	Instructor's Comments

STYLE 3

Date	Grade	Instructor	Instructor's Comments

STYLE 4

Date	Grade	Instructor	Instructor's Comments

STYLE 5

Date	Grade	Instructor	Instructor's Comments

STYLE 6

Date	Grade	Instructor	Instructor's Comments

STYLE 7

Date	Grade	Instructor	Instructor's Comments

STYLE 8

Date	Grade	Instructor	Instructor's Comments

STYLE 9

Date	Grade	Instructor	Instructor's Comments

STYLE 10

Date	Grade	Instructor	Instructor's Comments

STYLE 11

Date	Grade	Instructor	Instructor's Comments

STYLE 12

Date	Grade	Instructor	Instructor's Comments

STYLE 13

Date	Grade	Instructor	Instructor's Comments

STYLE 14

Date	Grade	Instructor	Instructor's Comments

STYLE 15

Date	Grade	Instructor	Instructor's Comments